Baroque Charted Designs for Needlework

Baroque Charted Designs for Needlework

Engraved by
Johan Sibmacher

Dover Publications, Inc., New York

TRANSLATION OF ORIGINAL TITLE PAGE

New pattern book engraved on copper, containing all sorts of new patterns of thinly, medium and thickly cut-out work and other artistic needlework, diligently published with the printing privilege of the Holy Roman Emperor, Nuremberg, 1604.

Published in Canada by General Publishing Company, Ltd., 30 Lesmill Road, Don Mills, Toronto, Ontario.
Published in the United Kingdom by Constable and Company, Ltd., 10 Orange Street, London WC 2.

This Dover edition, first published in 1975, is an unabridged republication of the 1880 edition of *Newes Modelbuch . . . . Inn Druck verfertigt,* a work originally published in Nuremberg in 1604. The 1880 edition was published by Ernst Wasmuth in Berlin in 1880 under the title *Kreuzstich-Muster, 36 Tafeln der Ausgabe v. 1604* ("Cross-Stitch Patterns, 36 Plates of the 1604 Edition.")
This edition contains new translations of the original 1604 title page and dedication.

International Standard Book Number: 0-486-23186-0
Library of Congress Catalog Card Number: 75-2820

Manufactured in the United States of America
Dover Publications, Inc.
180 Varick Street
New York, N.Y. 10014

Newes
Modelbüch In Kupffer
gemacht. Darinen aller hand Arth Newer
Mödel von Dün Mittel vnd Dick auß geschni
dener Arbeit auch andem Künstlichen Neh
werck zü gebrauchen. mit vleiß Inn
Druck verfertigt
Mit Röm: Kay: May: Freyheit.

Nürnberg.
M.D. CIIII

The picture was drawn and engraved by Johan Sibmacher. The ladies represent, from left to right, Wisdom, Diligence and Idleness. The homely rhyme may be translated:

> Let her who cares for needlework,
> And wishes to perform the same,
> Learn thoroughly and never shirk,
> And she'll obtain both praise and fame.

The roman numerals above the plates indicate the number of vertical meshes *(Gänge)* in the designs.

XXXXXIII.

XXXI.

4

XXIII.

LXVII.

XXXXVII.

XXXXVIII.

LXVII.

XXXV.

7

XXXXIII.

XXVII.

Mitt xxv Hengen.

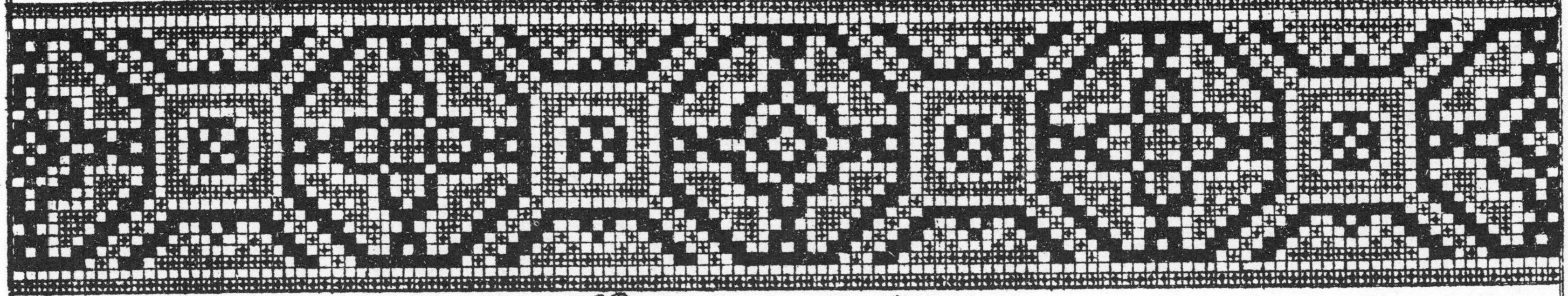

Mitt xxxxx. Hengen.

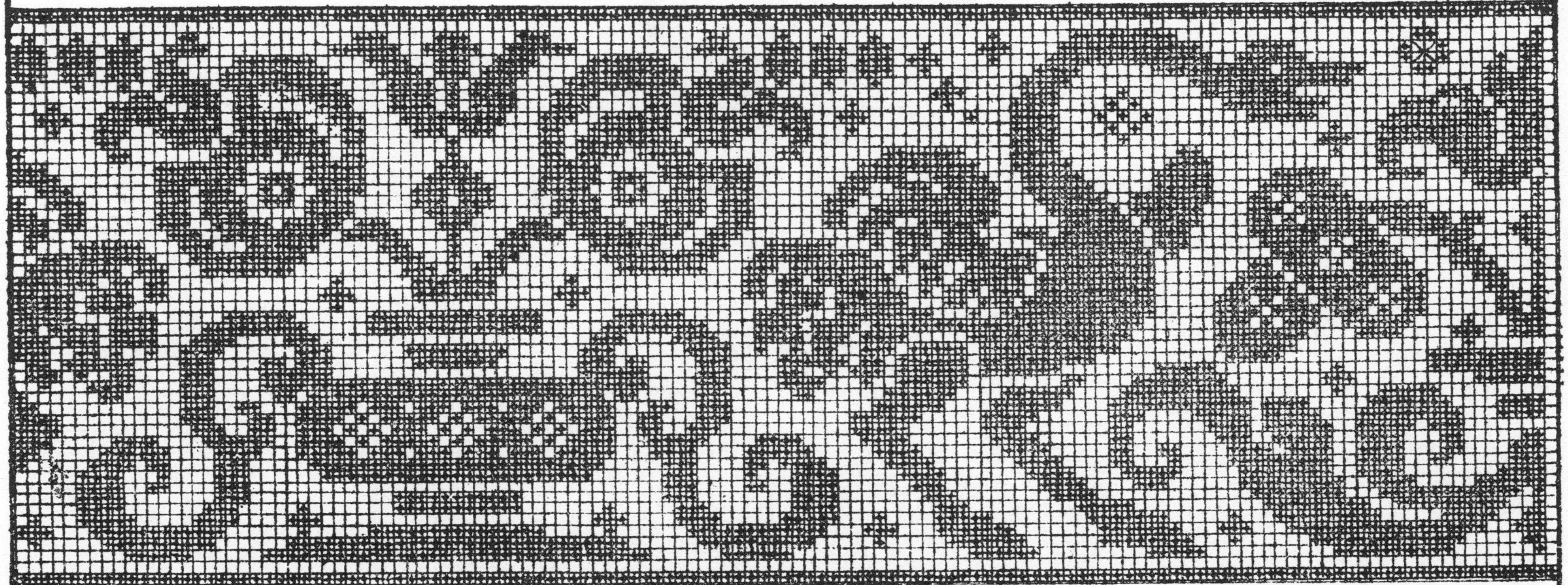

Mitt xiii Hengen.

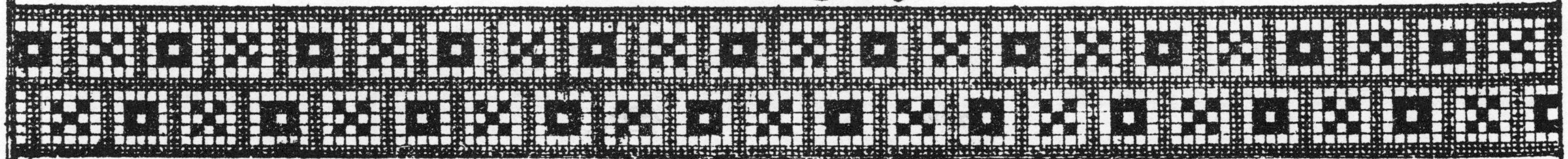

14.

XXXXXIII.

XXXXI.

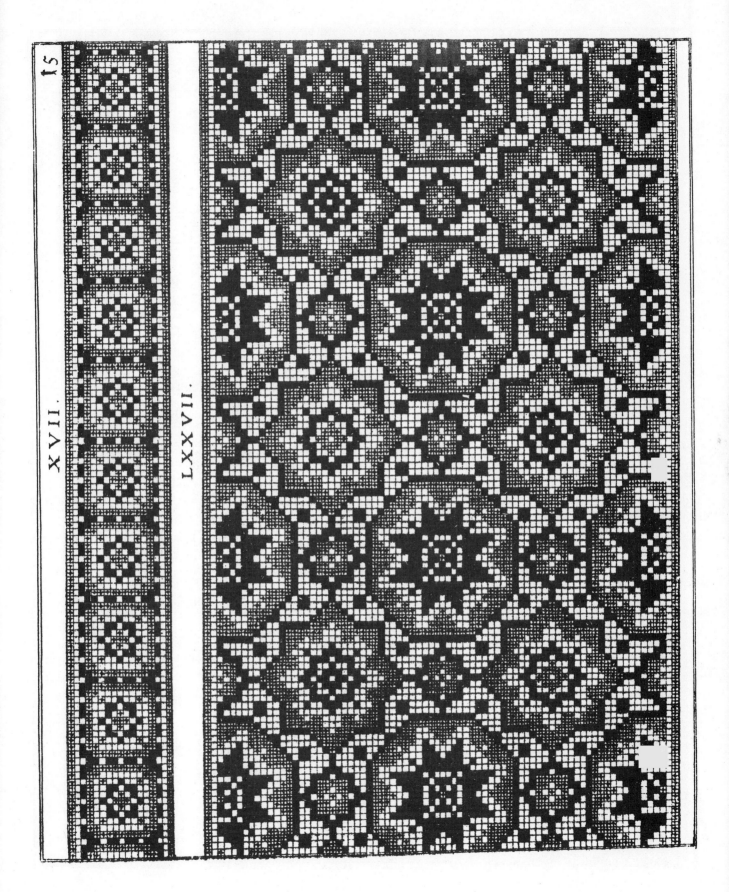

XVII.

LXXVII.

XXXVII.

XXXXVIIII.

LXVI.

XXV.

Blatt xxvii Gengen.

Blatt LXV. Gengen.

49

Mit XXXXIII Venngen.

Mit XXXXX. Venngen.

22

XXXXVIIII.

XVIIII.

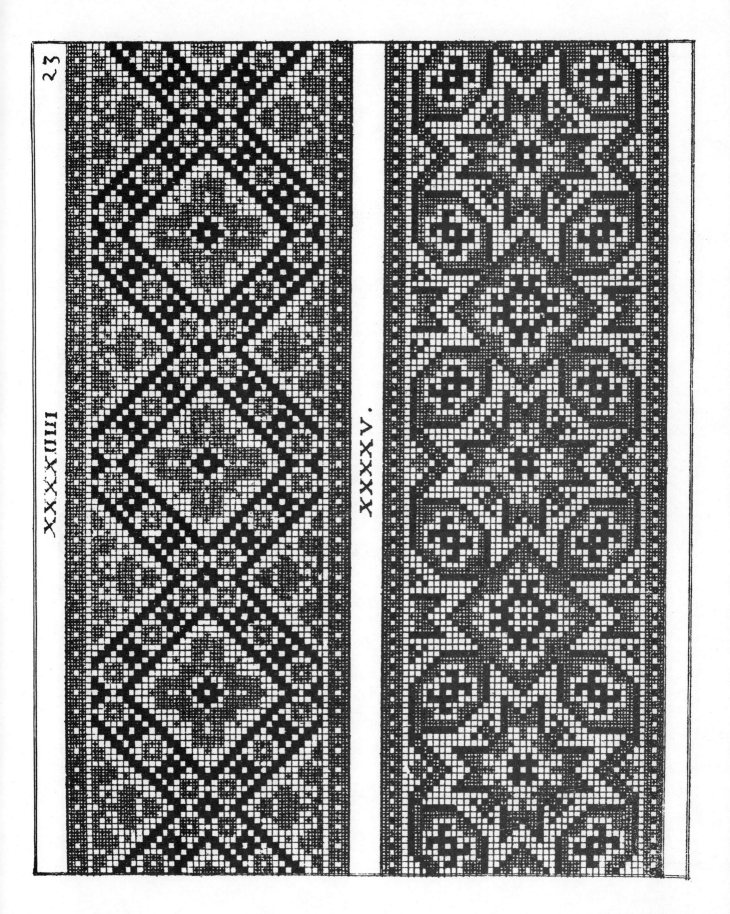

23

XXXXVIIII

XXXXV.

24

XXXXXV.

XXVI.

LXVII.

XXI.

25

26

XXXXIIII.

XXXXXV.

XXXXII.

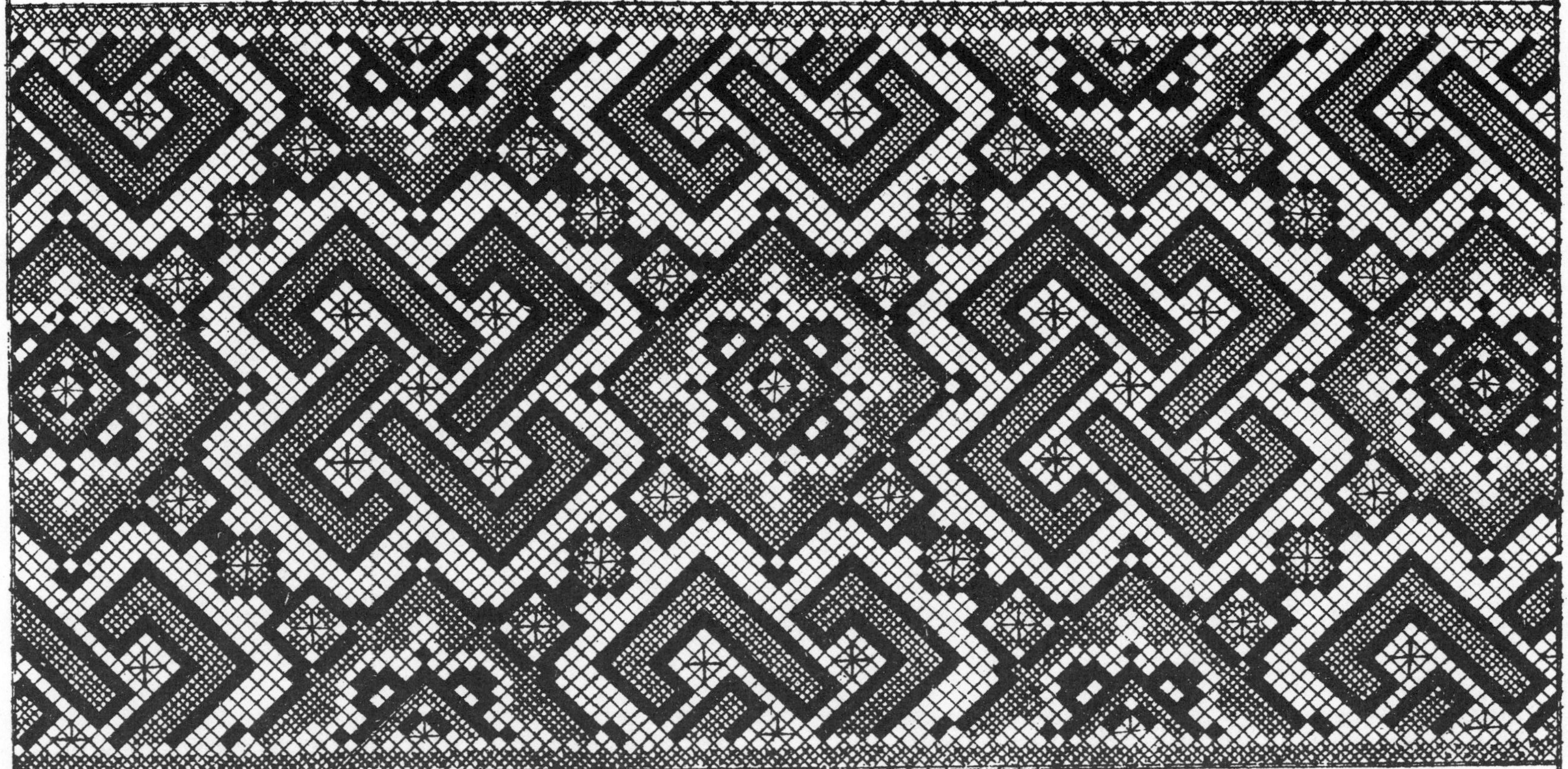

XXVI

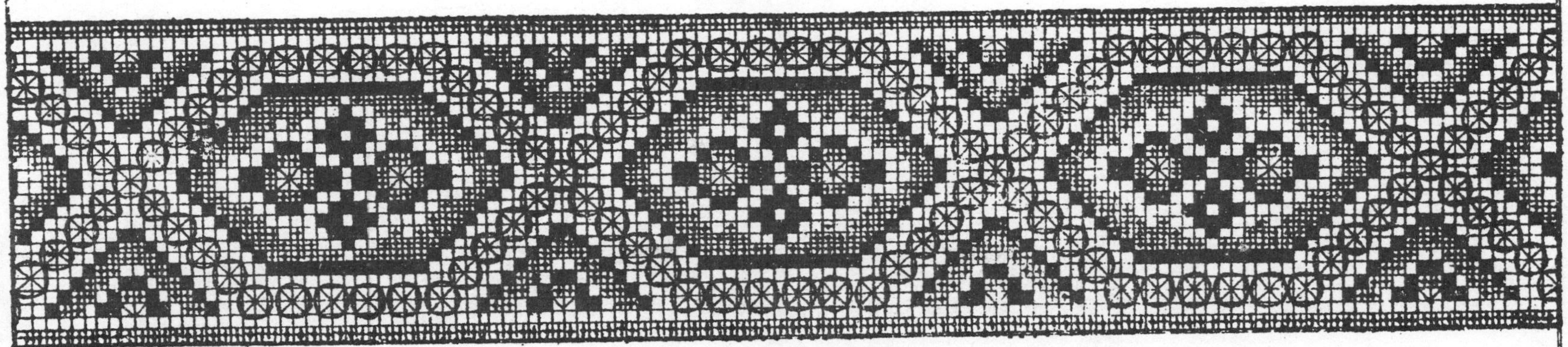

XXXV.

XXXVIIII.

LXXXI.

29

30

LXXXI.

31.

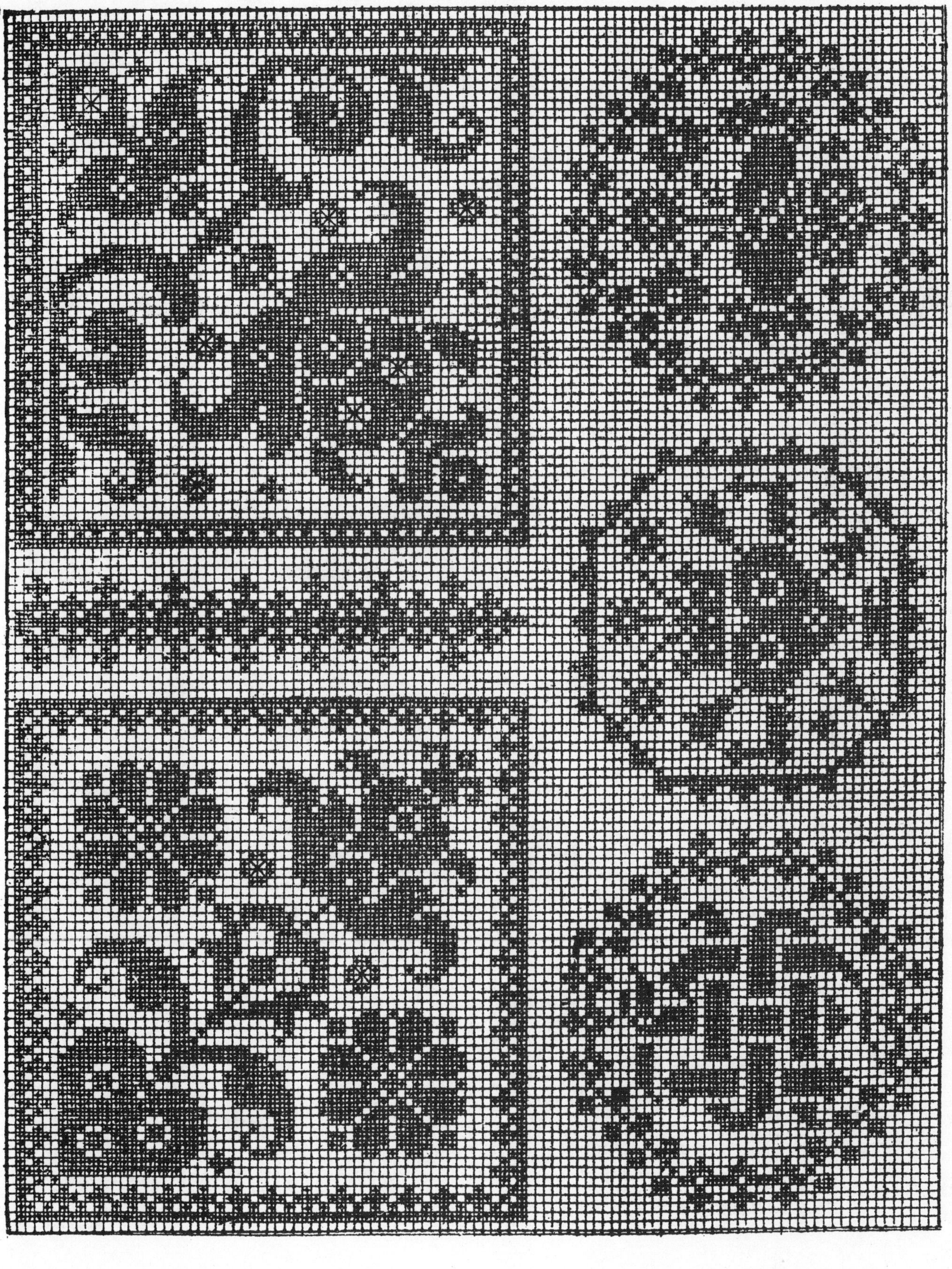

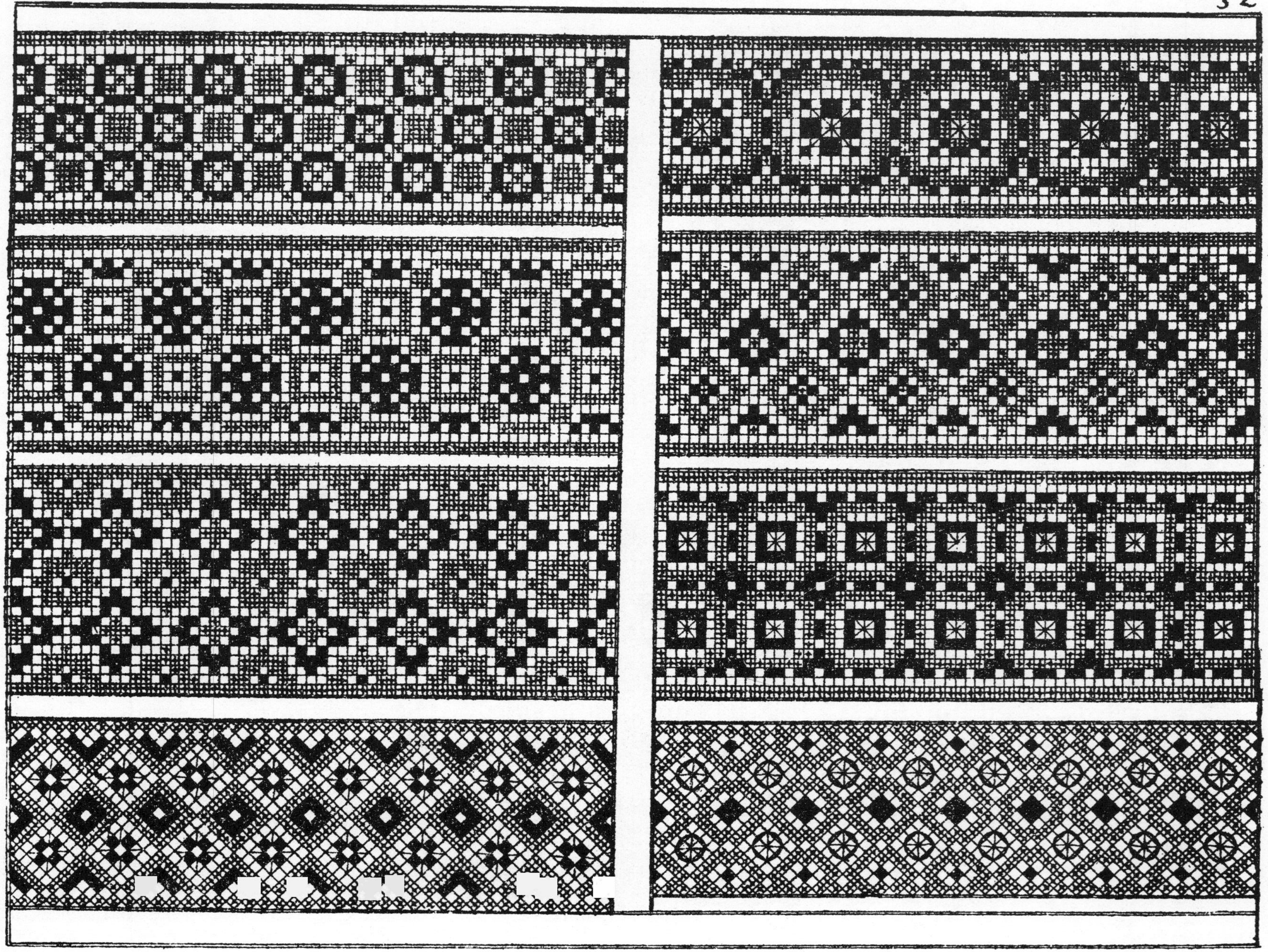

33

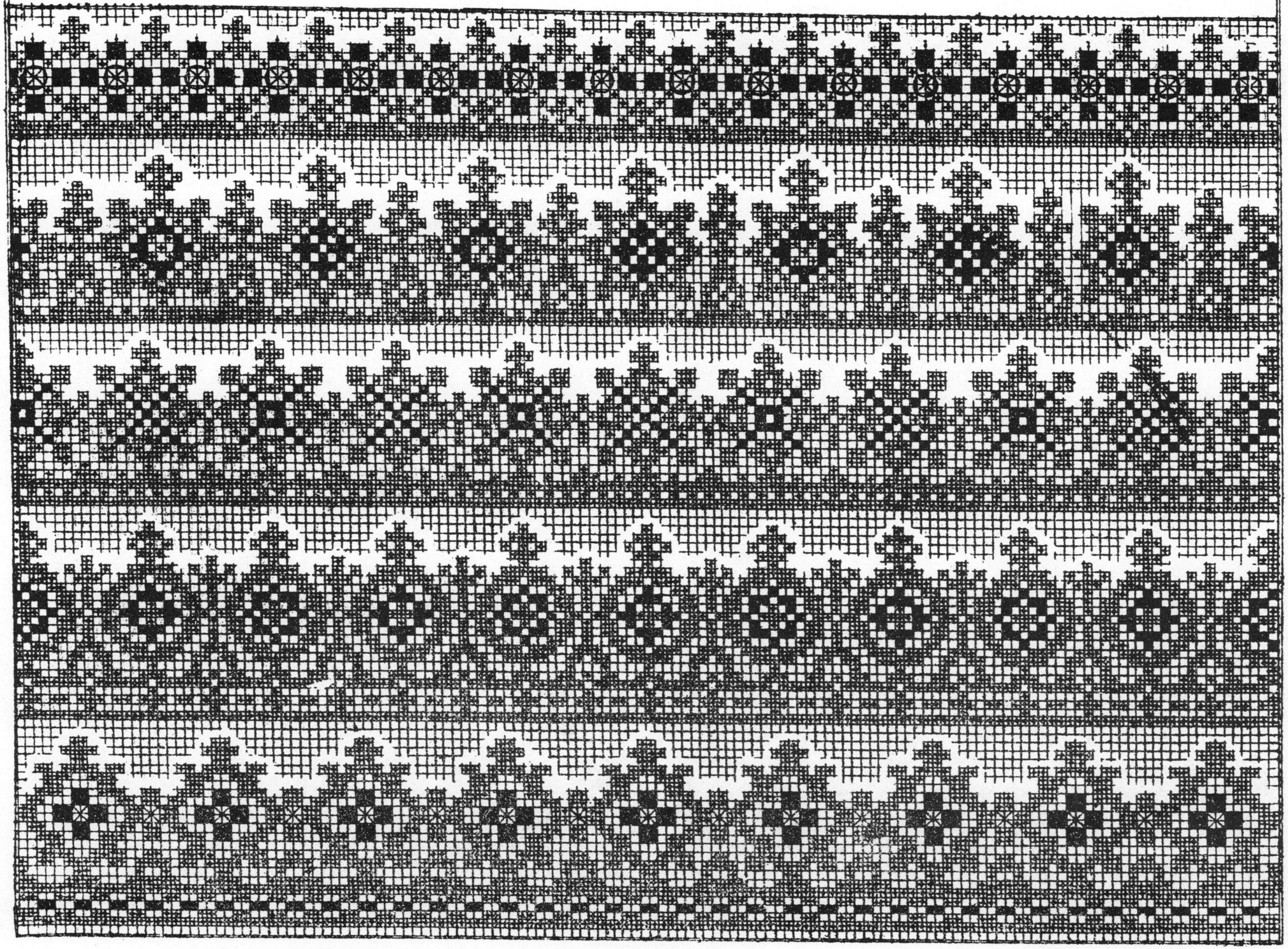

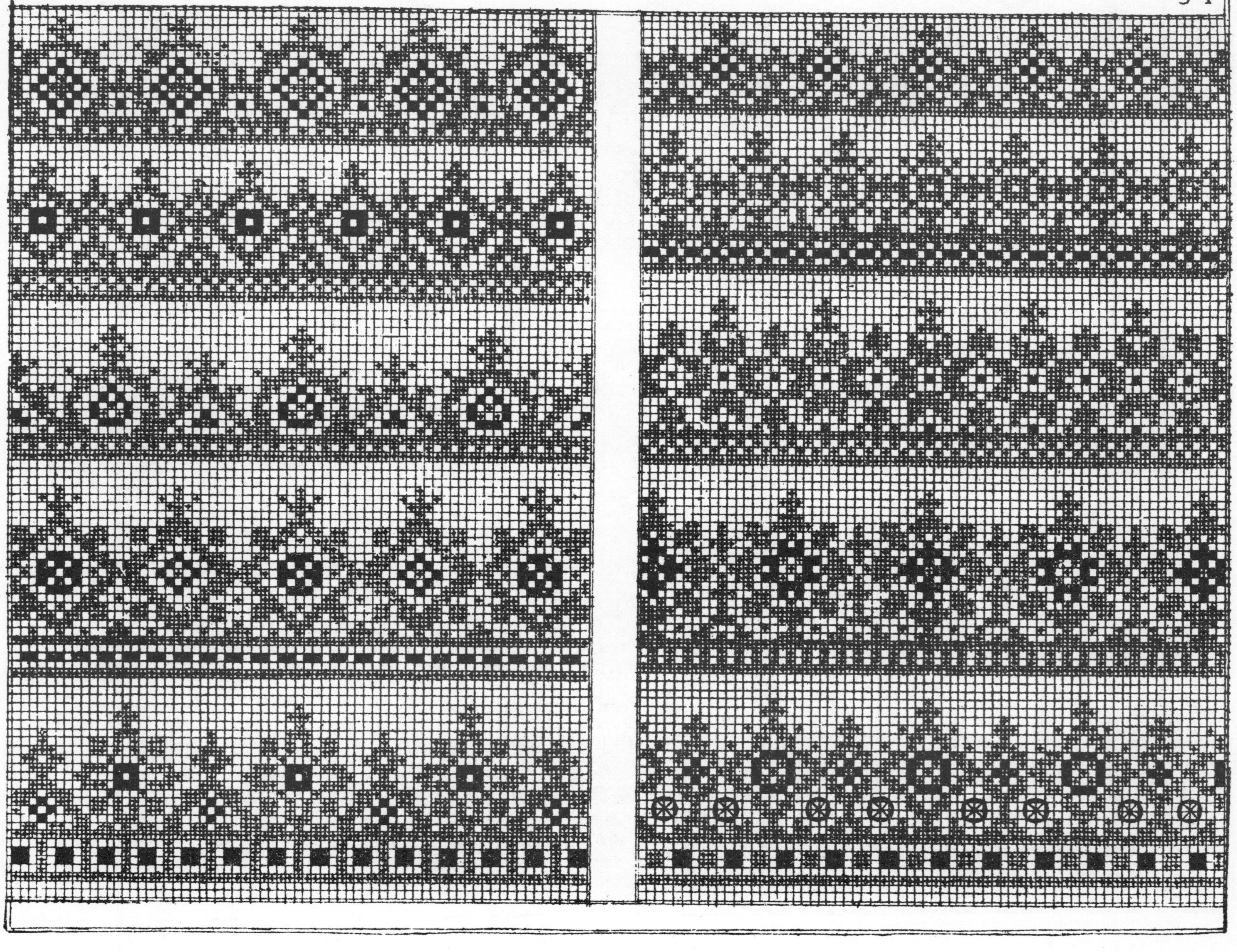